INTRODUCTION

I0499179

The format of the case review template is intentionally compact to help you keep your briefs just that - brief. However, if you need additional space, consider purchasing the digital version, which is available on the publisher's website.

Read a case once through before writing your brief. Use different colored highlighters or pens to annotate the case as you read. Then complete each section of the template:

Case

Write the case name and citation, then add it to the table of contents for easy reference.

Issue(s)

Determine what legal questions that the court was asked to answer, formatting each issue as a yes/no question.

Facts

List the people involved in the case, their actions, and any relevant locations, dates, and objects.

Holding & Rationale

The holding is the court's ruling; make note of any dissenting opinions when present. The rationale for the ruling should include any "Black Letter Law" (established precedents and standards that are undisputed) used to justify the ruling.

Analysis

Evaluate the significance of the case, its relationship to other cases, and the impact it had on litigants, government, or society. Your analysis could also include any personal commentary.

Notes

The blank notes page can be used to take notes during class, or to include additional information such as procedural history.

For a digital version and other academic notebooks, visit our website at phrontisterypublishing.com

Copyright 2019 Phrontistery Publishing, All Rights Reserved.

TABLE OF CONTENTS

CASE NAME	PAGE

CASE NAME	PAGE

TABLE OF CONTENTS

CASE NAME	PAGE

CASE:

ISSUE(S)

FACTS

HOLDING & RATIONALE

ANALYSIS

CASE:

ISSUE(S)

FACTS

HOLDING & RATIONALE

ANALYSIS

CASE:

ISSUE(S)

FACTS

HOLDING & RATIONALE

ANALYSIS

CASE:

ISSUE(S)

FACTS

HOLDING & RATIONALE

ANALYSIS

CASE:

ISSUE(S)

FACTS

HOLDING & RATIONALE

ANALYSIS

CASE:

ISSUE(S)

FACTS

HOLDING & RATIONALE

ANALYSIS

CASE:

ISSUE(S)

FACTS

HOLDING & RATIONALE

ANALYSIS

CASE:

ISSUE(S)

FACTS

HOLDING & RATIONALE

ANALYSIS

CASE:

ISSUE(S)

FACTS

HOLDING & RATIONALE

ANALYSIS

CASE:

ISSUE(S)

FACTS

HOLDING & RATIONALE

ANALYSIS

CASE:

ISSUE(S)

FACTS

HOLDING & RATIONALE

ANALYSIS

CASE:

ISSUE(S)

FACTS

HOLDING & RATIONALE

ANALYSIS

CASE:

ISSUE(S)

FACTS

HOLDING & RATIONALE

ANALYSIS

CASE:

ISSUE(S)

FACTS

HOLDING & RATIONALE

ANALYSIS

CASE:

ISSUE(S)

FACTS

HOLDING & RATIONALE

ANALYSIS

CASE:

ISSUE(S)

FACTS

HOLDING & RATIONALE

ANALYSIS

CASE:

ISSUE(S)

FACTS

HOLDING & RATIONALE

ANALYSIS

CASE:

ISSUE(S)

FACTS

HOLDING & RATIONALE

ANALYSIS

CASE:

ISSUE(S)

FACTS

HOLDING & RATIONALE

ANALYSIS

CASE:

ISSUE(S)

FACTS

HOLDING & RATIONALE

ANALYSIS

CASE:

ISSUE(S)

FACTS

HOLDING & RATIONALE

ANALYSIS

CASE:

ISSUE(S)

FACTS

HOLDING & RATIONALE

ANALYSIS

CASE:

ISSUE(S)

FACTS

HOLDING & RATIONALE

ANALYSIS

CASE:

ISSUE(S)

FACTS

HOLDING & RATIONALE

ANALYSIS

CASE:

FACTS

HOLDING & RATIONALE

ANALYSIS

CASE:

ISSUE(S)

FACTS

HOLDING & RATIONALE

ANALYSIS

CASE:

ISSUE(S)

FACTS

HOLDING & RATIONALE

ANALYSIS

CASE:

ISSUE(S)

FACTS

HOLDING & RATIONALE

ANALYSIS

CASE:

ISSUE(S)

FACTS

HOLDING & RATIONALE

ANALYSIS

CASE:

ISSUE(S)

FACTS

HOLDING & RATIONALE

ANALYSIS

CASE:

ISSUE(S)

FACTS

HOLDING & RATIONALE

ANALYSIS

CASE:

ISSUE(S)

FACTS

HOLDING & RATIONALE

ANALYSIS

CASE:

ISSUE(S)

FACTS

HOLDING & RATIONALE

ANALYSIS

CASE:

ISSUE(S)

FACTS

HOLDING & RATIONALE

ANALYSIS

CASE:

ISSUE(S)

FACTS

HOLDING & RATIONALE

ANALYSIS

CASE:

ISSUE(S)

FACTS

HOLDING & RATIONALE

ANALYSIS

CASE:

ISSUE(S)

FACTS

HOLDING & RATIONALE

ANALYSIS

CASE:

ISSUE(S)

FACTS

HOLDING & RATIONALE

ANALYSIS

CASE:

ISSUE(S)

FACTS

HOLDING & RATIONALE

ANALYSIS

CASE:

ISSUE(S)

FACTS

HOLDING & RATIONALE

ANALYSIS

CASE:

ISSUE(S)

FACTS

HOLDING & RATIONALE

ANALYSIS

CASE:

ISSUE(S)

FACTS

HOLDING & RATIONALE

ANALYSIS

CASE:

ISSUE(S)

FACTS

HOLDING & RATIONALE

ANALYSIS

CASE:

ISSUE(S)

FACTS

HOLDING & RATIONALE

ANALYSIS

CASE:

ISSUE(S)

FACTS

HOLDING & RATIONALE

ANALYSIS

CASE:

ISSUE(S)

FACTS

HOLDING & RATIONALE

ANALYSIS

CASE:

ISSUE(S)

FACTS

HOLDING & RATIONALE

ANALYSIS

CASE:

ISSUE(S)

FACTS

HOLDING & RATIONALE

ANALYSIS

CASE:

ISSUE(S)

FACTS

HOLDING & RATIONALE

ANALYSIS

CASE:

ISSUE(S)

FACTS

HOLDING & RATIONALE

ANALYSIS

www.ingramcontent.com/pod-product-compliance
Lightning Source LLC
Chambersburg PA
CBHW082018230526
45466CB00022B/2488